The Attitude Of Love
The Power Within You

By: Sylvia Myers

Copyright © 2013 Sylvia Myers
All rights reserved.

ISBN: 0989433501
ISBN-13: 9780989433501

Table of Contents

Attitude Defined	1
Attitude opposite Energy: Turpitude	3
Life is a TEST of Lessons in Love	5
An attitude of Love	9
God's Attitude of Love	11
God's Attitude toward sin	13
The Crossroad of "MUST"	17
Alignment	19
Preparation	21

ATTITUDE DEFINED

What is Attitude?
ATTITUDE – It is the gasoline that runs through our thoughts and belief system. It is the energy that runs through everything we think, feel, believe, and it is always flowing.

One is never disconnected from attitude; because, attitude is always present within you. Attitude is saturated in each spiritual being. Your own authentic attitude is your true self, your exclusive rhythm in the universe.

Each authentic attitude is embodied by a soul, when this authenticity manifests, it is always a work of art. You are a masterpiece, with the authentic signature of God -your Creator.

Attitude is an energy that travels through the spirit of man, embodies the soul of man, and is present in the physical man. Throughout the remainder of the book, attitude and energy are used synonymously.

In every moment, you have the authority and power to choose. The power of your choice is the authority God gave you for your life. Inside of every thought, decision and action is energy. This energy or attitude is present in whatever you believe or don't believe. Your attitude determines your ability (can do) or your inability (cannot do) to succeed or persevere through life's challenging moments. Your attitude is a determining factor in how long it takes you to manifest your goals. It is an ever present, circulating force that is with us whether we recognize it or not.

You are always operating in your own/individual choosing. There is only one "you" and everything about you is unique.

When one makes a choice, attitude is always present. A GOD (LOVE) attitude is comprised of the following three parts:
1. Attitude of the spirit/heart- enlightenment, intuition, a knowing, discernment
2. Attitude of the mind/soul- emotions, desire, will, intellect
3. Attitude of the body/physical realm – what you see, smell, taste, touch, feel

The Attitude of Love is: the fruit of Love's attitude is harvested when these things are present: compassion, long-suffering, giving totally of one's self to serve others, joy, peace, patience, kindness, goodness, faithfulness, gentleness, self-discipline and divine power. Attitude dwells within each of us (spiritually) and manifests itself through our actions (physically).

ATTITUDE OPPOSITE ENERGY:
Turpitude

TURPITUDE – It is the exact opposite of attitude; the opposite of love.

We can think of turpitude as: evil thoughts, theft, murder, adultery, sexual immorality, greed, wickedness, deceit, envy, slander, pride, foolishness, vileness and depravity. Simply put, turpitude is anything that causes emotional suffering or discontentment in another person. It presents itself in our day-to-day lives as jealousy, gossip, confusion, negativity, self-righteousness, judgment, hate, ignorance and closed mindedness. The unawareness of truth and choosing not to discover your real identity displays itself as turpitude. It is selfishness and the inability to recognize that we are all connected to one another. Turpitude is not the core base of any person because we are created in the image of God, according to Genesis 1:27. If you act within the energy of turpitude, it is by choice.

LIFE IS A TEST
of Lessons in Love

A farmer went out to sow his seed. As he was scattering the seed, some fell along the path, and the birds came and ate it up. Some fell on rocky places, where it did not have much soil. It sprang up quickly, because the soil was shallow. But when the sun came up, the plants were scorched, and they withered because they had no root. Other seed fell among thorns, which grew up and choked the plants. Still other seed fell on good soil, where it produced a crop — a hundred, sixty or thirty times what was sown.
-Matthew 13:3-8 NIV

Listen then to what the parable of the sower means: When anyone hears the message about the kingdom and does not understand it, the evil one comes and snatches away what was sown in his heart. This is the seed sown along the path. The one who received the seed that fell on rocky places is the man who hears the word and at once receives it with joy. But since he has no root, he lasts only a short time. When trouble or persecution comes because of the word, he quickly falls away. The one who received the seed that fell among the thorns is the man who hears the word, but the worries of this life and the deceitfulness of wealth choke it, making it unfruitful. But the one who received the seed that fell on good soil is the man who hears the word and understands it. He produces a crop, yielding a hundred, sixty or thirty times what was sown.
-Matthew 13:18-23 NIV

The four soils represent the four categories of one's spiritual (inward) growth. Each soil can only respond to the level of development it has within it. So, to the degree in which one's attitude of love is developed, to that exact degree one will sow and reap in his/her life.

Every circumstance, situation, temptation is allowed and will cause the evolution of Christ-Consciousness, which is the awareness of truth in love.

Only when you choose to love all matters, (rather positive or negative) waters the incorruptible seed within you. The secret to manifesting God's best in your life is in your attitude of love. Therefore, choose an attitude of love, and the consequences are no weapon formed against you can prosper.

Challenges of life are a necessary; it is usually through our trying moments where our faith and resolve are tested. It is also in those moments that we lean (or should lean) on God's love. Leaning on God's love during those times is a practice of "long-suffering." When a person hears the Word of God or a Spiritual Principle of Truth from the Universe, but it does not take root, the challenges of life can become overwhelming and a situation that could have been used for growth of character instead becomes a moment consumed in your own despair.

When one becomes distracted from the Attitude of Love, a shift occurs. This shift causes a disconnection to those around you and an increase in self-absorption. Often times, distractions are: self pleasures and usually beautiful or appealing in appearance. If one continues in this turpitude and selfishness, those distractions then become pleasurable habits and those habits then become mental and physical enslaving addictions. Other distractions are giving too much attention to matters of the past or future; instead of being present in each moment, not realizing that now, all your needs are met. Rather, be thankful in each moment and acknowledge your current blessings. All distractions are walking in ignorance of the Divine Love Nature, which is within us.

The truth of the matter is: we are all one human family and need each and every authentic self to manifest in our world. Re-center on the Word of God, on Love, on an attitude of Love. Growth in character is developed in an Attitude of Love. As you trust Love - patience, steadfastness, peace and joy emerges from within you in any situation. Practice this exercise- when reading the Word of God, every place you read 'God' replace it with 'Love'.

Then [LOVE] said, "Let us make people" in our image, to be like ourselves. They will be masters over all life – the fish in the sea, the birds in the sky, and all the livestock, wild animals, and small animals.
So [LOVE] created people in His own image; [LOVE] patterned them after Himself; male and female He created them.

Genesis 1:26-27 NKJV

God is loving and responsible and personal in providing for each authentic being. You are love created by Love for Love. Since God is Love, and we are created in His image then we are spiritual beings created by Love for Love; therefore, we MUST love in everything we do. Why do you think every human being desires love? Here is a universal desire that all humans share! Every being in the universe desires the love connection. We are to imitate Love in our thinking, speaking, acting....which is manifesting God's authentic attitude of the heart: the Attitude of Love.

Life's tests challenge us to choose to love in moments of life when people or circumstances offend us. If we journey as we ought, we love in those negative moments; that is what will make the difference in your life and those around you. To pass the challenges and walk in the opportunities afforded to you each day, simply love. (Remember, you are constantly choosing... will you choose an attitude of love or turpitude of hate?)

Attitude is so powerful, it impacts the way you think of yourself. Attitude changes your atmosphere. Attitude is a powerful energy that goes unrecognized for the dynamite that it is. When you operate in turpitude you get stuck in a negative energy bubble. Often times stuck on unimportant matters. I call it "stuck on petty". Most offenses are petty. The next time you get upset or bothered in a negative way; do the "petty test" on yourself. Here is how to administer the "petty test": Simply ask yourself this question: If I were to die today, does this circumstance or event really matter? If not, then don't get "stuck on petty." Avoid the petty by reminding yourself of your purpose for being; you are a creation of love. Remember that everyone has a common design and that is to flow or journey in an attitude of love, in every moment. This is an opportunity to live out your purpose. Whatever your decision is, attitude or turpitude, will be exactly what you get back. In the entire universe, there is only ONE truth and that is the Word of God. Colossians 1:17 says that by the Word of God, everything we see was created and is held together. It is by the Word of Love that we live and have our being.

Let attitude be your consistent service or gift to the world around you. Your own authentic attitude is the God in you being expressed artistically. You have the attitude of Jesus Christ which was given to you through His resurrection. Attitude comes from God. Let me say that again- attitude comes from Love. To develop Love-Mindedness, you MUST apply the Word of God. When faced with a difficult situation, set your mind on the Word of Love. Remember that all circumstances are temporary; they will change. Operate in Love's authority and choose to speak the Word of Truth to that situation. Choose to think the Word of Truth. Choose to act in love at all times, in every situation. This is how you apply the Word of God to your life. When you develop Love thoughts, you will have Love actions. If you follow all of these steps, you are permitting the attitude of Love to flow from your authentic self. And that's exactly what the world, you, and the people around you need.

Food for thought:
- If you only said loving things about the people around you (or said nothing at all), would there be a different energy surrounding you?
- If you only thought loving thoughts, what attitude would continuously flow from you and within you?
- What would happen if you chose to focus on the positive in a situation rather than the negative?
- What energy would be created if you did not speak negativity to your current circumstance, but instead kept silent?

AN ATTITUDE OF LOVE

God is the purpose and meaning for everything of worth. He is Life; the significance of all things. He is the hope in all matters, situations, and circumstances. Live life in Love's purpose. Knowing your purpose causes you to focus your entire being on Him. Thus, one is flowing in attitude- birthing and giving the world the real you, authentically.

Attitude is a form of worship. Mark 12:30 reads "love the LORD your God with all your heart, with all your soul, with your entire mind, and with all your strength."

Question: How do you love God with your body?

Answer: When you exercise your body, the attitude you exercise in determines how well you enjoyed that work-out OR how much you dreaded exercising.

Mark 12: 31 instruct us to, "Love your neighbor as yourself." Loving your neighbor consists of your attitude. Serving others in an attitude of love is communicated by the quality of service in which you yield to another individual.

Follow [LOVE's] example in everything you do, because you are His dear children. Live a life filled with love for others, following the example of [LOVE,] who loved you and gave Himself as a sacrifice to take away your sins.

Ephesians 5:1-2 NKJV

Walk or journey responding to the Love of God by imitating Him through an attitude of Love. Attitude is the gasoline that runs through thoughts, through emotions, through desires, through words, through actions.

Give thanks in all circumstances for this is the will of [Love] concerning you.

I Thessalonians 5:16 NKJV

When you have an attitude of gratitude you go forward, moving in a positive energy. Your attitude is your distinctive vehicle. It is a master influence on your life. It is clearly revealed by the words you speak; the tone of your voice, and evidenced by your daily conversation with others. Attitude is revealed in everything you do. When you encounter something, whether it be good or bad, do this- maintain an attitude of Love, in that moment. Then, watch how you feel about the situation and in time watch those circumstances concerning you channel back love to you. You control your entire world by surrendering to that attitude of Love. Whenever you surrender to an attitude of Love, you operate in uncontained power. There are no limits; there's nothing to suppress you. You are free.

Fear is a spiritual energy with mental, emotional, and physical consequences that negatively impact us. Choosing to operate in fear puts one in containment or a prison. I John 4:18 tells us that, "There is no fear in love; but perfect love casts out fear." Can you imagine this, living without fear? Attitude of Love is total power and self control. The attitude of Love conquers ALL. Choosing to operate in an attitude of Love makes you fearless. You walk in complete assurance when you walk in Love. Journey in Love and walk divinely, with confidence, from your spirit.

GOD'S ATTITUDE OF LOVE

God's obvious attitude is creation was and is one of authority. God decided to create us in His image; thus putting us in authority over the physical realm.

>Then God said, "Let us make man in our image, in our likeness, and let them rule over the fish of the sea and the birds of the air, over the livestock, over all the earth, and over all the creatures that move along the ground."
>-Genesis 1:26 Life Application Bible

God has authorized us to command, delegate, to rule over this world. Love provides us with complete authority by making us gods and that has not changed.

>God blessed them and said to them, "Be fruitful and increase in number; fill the earth and subdue it. Rule over the fish of the sea and the birds of the air and over every living creature that moves on the ground."
>-Genesis 1:28 Life Application Bible

God's attitude is abundance for everyone and everything.

>Then God said, "I give you every seed-bearing plant on the face of the whole earth and every tree that has fruit with seed in it. They will be your for food. And to all the beasts of the earth and all the birds of the air and all the creatures that move on the ground – EVERYTHING that has breath of life in it – I give every green plant for food. And it was so.
>-Genesis 1:29-30 Life Application Bible

God's attitude is loving and generous to every living thing that was created. Love said, "I give YOU every seed-bearing plant on the face of the whole earth."

God spoke to Adam and every seed in Adam.

God's attitude is one of complete and total provision to everyone; you, me and all the creatures that dwell on earth.

GOD'S ATTITUDE TOWARD SIN

Then man and his wife heard the sound of the Lord God as He was walking in the garden in the cool of the day, and they hid from the Lord God among the trees of the garden.

But the Lord God called to the man, "Where are you?"

Adam answered, "I heard You in the garden, and I was afraid because I was naked; so I hid."

-Genesis 3:8-10 Life Application Bible

LET'S PAUSE FOR A MOMENT TO DISCUSS ADAM'S ATTITUDE

Adam's attitude was one of fear of God seeing him naked. Adam did not fear God because of his disobedience.

No, Adam's attitude reflected the truth about God's loving character as Creator. It show Adam did not fear the One who was His Friend.

Adam's attitude prove he KNEW LOVE was NOT going to destroy him because of his failure or bad decision. Adam hid because he simply did not want Him to see his naked body.

Adam's only reply to God was "I heard you, so I hid, because I am naked"

Adam's only focused on the physical realm. This is where our human family get stuck – IN THE PHYSICAL REALM, on the natural circumstances.

LET'S RETURN TO EXPERIENCING GOD'S ATTITUDE OF LOVE TOWARD US

And God said "Who told you that you were naked? Have you eaten from the tree that I commanded you not to eat from?"

The man said, "The woman you put here with me – she gave me some fruit from the tree, and I ate it."

> Then the Lord God said to the woman, "What is this you have done?"
> The woman said, "The serpent deceived me, and I ate."
> So the Lord God said to the serpent, "Because you have done this, you will crawl on your belly and you will eat dust all the days of your life.
> AND I will put enmity between you and the woman, and between your offspring and hers, He will crush your head, and you will strike His heel.
> -Genesis 3:11-14 Life Application Bible

God's attitude was GRACE. He spoke of The Love Seed He was going to provide in that moment for the damage that was in place.

Love did not judge us – It sacrificed ITSELF for us.

-----Nothing comes from judgment

-----Nothing grow from judgment

-----Nothing thrives, flourishes, prospers in judgment

One will never judge another when they have the revelation of love; IF you judge you are absent of the essence of Love.

God's attitude despite the prevailing circumstances of Adam, Eve, the serpent, you, me is love. God's reaction was/is love, protection and provision; as IS His Attitude of Love right now and it has always been.

Ponder this: Have you ever been self destructive, disrespectful toward others and yourself; abusive, and verbally demeaning towards others and yourself, or completely failed and betrayed others and yourself.......only to become aware of His loving presence that bestowed healing, provision, restoration and reconcile you in whatever area of your life that needed it

ALL human beings are beautiful. Everything Love created is perfectly beautiful.

"[All of the things that challenge us are the things that complete us. Those are the things that mode us into who we are – perfection."

All random, seemingly coincident and disjointed pieces in one's life always miraculously come together to form one's original master plan – "destiny."

Every part, every moment, every situation and event forms into – One Plan…His Story in your creation – your history is His planned destiny and everything He created is Perfection.]"

Love is the answer to all things; only love can make all things perfectly beautiful.

For God was in Christ, reconciling the world to Himself, no longer counting people's sins against them. And He gave us this wonderful message of reconciliation.

-2 Corinthians 5:19 New Living Translation

THE CROSSROADS OF "MUST"

At some point, in everyone's life, you reach a crossroads called "MUST". This is when your life must change paths. Circumstances and events occur, thus pressing you to do something different; urging you to change the present course you are on. To change, we MUST learn that we are spirit beings and our world is spiritual. Although we are spirit beings, we usually mosey through life unaware. We tend to focus only on what's concrete in front of us- the physical realm. This must change. We must realize we are spirit beings and everything we do is spiritual, yet we do not realize this truth. Our words are spiritual, and the words we speak bring us life or death.

FOR EXAMPLE:

***Once when I was a teen, there was a girl in my neighborhood who was the class clown. Nearly every day in class, she would raise her hand and tell the teacher, "I need to go to the counselor's office because I am deeply troubled. I am a drug dealer and I am a homosexual. I need help." Well, the teacher would excuse her to go get counseling from the school's counselor.

Now, this was a private, religious school. The girl only did this to skip class and to make the class laugh, because she was, in fact, not selling drugs. However, when I saw her in my early twenties, she was a drug dealer, a homosexual and was deeply troubled. The power of her words manifested and she was only kidding around…***

The daily decisions we make are spiritual. Again, we have the power to choose life or death because the decisions we make today are the prophecy of our future. Hearing is spiritual. Romans 10:17 states, "faith comes by hearing, and hearing by the word of God." When we pay attention or listen it is spiritual. We are spirit beings that are created in the image of God. God speaks things into existence. The greatest miracle in the world is the truth that God created everything we see out of nothing, by speaking it into existence. God sees the end from the beginning. The passion, talent and ability each person has are spiritual. Look at the results of passions...

Here are the results of their passions: EVERYTHING we use, on a daily basis, is the result of what another human being created through his/her passion.

FOR EXAMPLE:

One person desired to create an engine. Another person desired to create the wheel; and another a leather seat; another a radio; a steeling wheel and so on and so forth. At the end culmination of each of those passions, we all get to enjoy "THE CAR". So you see everything we use in our day-to-day is the manifestation of God's talent in each of us and it serves everyone's needs and wants. Think of anything: furniture, toothpaste, soap, canned goods, toilet tissue, running water, transportation, streets, highways, television, music, sports, a bed, clothing, electricity, etc... Your creative gift is spiritual. It serves the world as needed.

> Man does not live on bread alone, but by every Word that proceed from The Mouth of God...
>
> Matthew 4:4 NKJV
>
> The Spirit gives life; the flesh counts for nothing. The words I have spoken to you are spirit and they are life.
>
> John 6:63 NIV

Communication is spiritual...prayer is you and God communicating. It is you and LOVE talking and listening to each another. Do this: speak and believe only what God says about a matter, which is only truth, and watch the outcome of the matter. God's Word is Spirit and Life. The Word of Truth is spirit with total authority. All of these are examples that we are spirit beings operating in a physical realm. Jesus Christ ONLY lived and operated from His spirit while living in a natural, physical world. For us to operate successfully from the spiritual realm, we must grasp that we are to journey from the inside out. Not attending exclusively to the physical realm. Spiritually, we are to speak the Word of God's truth to that situation and believe it. When we align with Love and cross the road of "MUST" we will walk without limits.

ALIGNMENT

Alignment to the Word of God is this: RESPECTING, HONORING, CONSIDERING what the written Word of God has said. For example, in your thoughts say, "Love said think on:

"Whatever is true, whatever is noble, whatever is right, whatever is pure, whatever is lovely, whatever is admirable – if anything is excellent or praiseworthy-think about such things. Whatever truth you have learned or received or observed in [LOVE,] put it into practice. And the God of peace will be with you.

Philippians 4:8-9 NKJV

So do not align your words with circumstances because your words go before you and you will follow your words. Your words have the power to create; therefore, align your words to God's Word – the Word of Love. Be persistent in aligning with the rhythm of the Universe which is LOVE. Do not speak of temporary events as if that is your destiny or the final outcome; therefore, only speak truth and the events will align with it. Remember all events change.

IF we choose to reverence, honor, respect, and consider LOVE in everything that we do, think and say, then we walk actively in a relationship with God. This is how to walk closely with God. This is how to imitate Love. This is intimacy with Love and it is continuous fellowship with your Creator. This is how to journey in truth and to live the life that Love created you to live.

PREPARATION

Love is preparing you for what He HAS prepared for you.
    Divine appointments, divine connections, divine guidance, divine assignments are all designed to prepare and propel us into God's perfect plan and purpose for our life in Love. Everything God has planned for you is custom-designed, exclusively for you… that's how deeply in love He is with you. Know this truth: Destiny will happen. In time, destiny will manifest what is meant to be and what was meant to be is already progressing, processing and evolving in your life.

    Divine appointments are dates, times and seasons in the natural realm set by the Creator. It is His perfect timing personally set and designed for you, all the while providing His perfect will for you at an appointed time. This is apparent in daily miracles.

    Divine connections are people, places, events, situations and circumstances that divinely connect you to His purpose and your exclusive plan for being.

    Divine truth is the Word of Love. Every person has a story that Love planned and purposed for you; a story filled with beauty because of His love for you.

    Divine guidance comes only to lead us into Love's desire for our journey. We must remain receptive to God's guidance, the teaching and leading of the Holy Spirit. Your intuition or a deep knowing within you is Divine guidance. I call it "the Voice of God". Divine guidance requires immediate obedience to the Word of God.

    Divine assignments are those passions or flames within your spirit that even during insurmountable circumstances, you continue to develop or evolve that desire. You persevere, you follow that passion and you end up giving the world your God given talents and gifts and abilities. When you do this, that divine assignment serves Love's purpose – which is your reason for being. Love wants you to be your real self.

    God is the only source and He expects us to be a resource. Jesus Christ is the way- our only way out and in. Jesus (the Word of God) is the Truth, my only truth into ALL things, the only truth in circumstances, events and situations.

> God has made everything beautiful for its own time or season. He has planted eternity in the human heart; but even so, people cannot see the whole scope of God's work from beginning to end.
>
> Ecclesiastes 3:11 NKJV

Get into alignment with God's mind (the Word of God) then His mind will be revealed and will manifest in your life. Manifest the purpose and plan that God has laid out for you by studying Truth – His Word. God said,

> "For we are (Love's) workmanship, created in Christ Jesus to do good works, which (Love)God prepared in advance for us to do"
>
> Ephesians 2:10 NKJV

Let me ask you a question…Did you ask to come here? Do you remember asking God to come here?

…yet here you are. So get busy discovering the paths that He planned for you. Discover His desires that are here for you by getting to know Him. Learn about Him, the way He thinks and the way He acts. Come to know His behavior. Learn His character. By doing this, you will discover your own authentic self. Your true self is His identity in you. What you will quickly discover is His divine nature is love; therefore, you are love. Think only what God thinks about all matters. We have to get a "God said" down in our spirit. "God said" is the only thing that counts. Live life in alignment with God, after all He manufactured you. We have to seek God's will regarding us. We MUST know the Voice of God. Develop a cultivating ear that knows "The Voice of God".

Here is an EXACT way to do this:

You must have a beginning, a fixed place or foundation. Now, you must trust in that foundation at all times and in every season of life journey.

You are a spirit being – you must move in that spirit realm while existing in this physical world. Rely solely on the Spirit within you. You are a divine being with a divine nature called love – ONLY LOVE in everything.

1. KNOW your true identity, THINK constantly about this truth – that you are a spirit being in a physical realm.

2. Come to understand how you were created and then you will understand the mighty power within you. You are a child of Almighty God,

and He – Himself dwells within you. Therefore, walk in complete freedom by remaining present in this awareness of truth.

3. Know your authentic self to be true. Follow those internal thoughts and ideas that come from within you.

4. Practice this …whatever you become aware of through Love's thoughts; believe it is the Spirit within communicating and leading you – then continue to put that inward awareness into outer practice.

This is how we walk in spiritual awareness or consciousness. The more you practice this, the deeper the manifestation of Spirit's presence will be in you, and the more love will dominate in your physical realm.

This is the truth about you:
The Lord God formed the man from the dust of the ground and breathed into his nostrils the breath of life, and the man became a living soul.
Genesis 2:7 NKJV

1. Man formed from the dust of the ground = Physical (body) being
2. And breathed into man nostril the breath of life = Spiritual (spirit) being
3. And man became a living soul = Soulical (soul) being

God formed man from the dust making man physical, and then breathed into man's nostril the breath of life, at that moment, spirit caused man to come to life. When the spirit entered the body that produced a living soul. The soul is your personality and individual self. The soul communicates with the spirit of man and the body of man. Some say it this way: spirit of man (the higher self), soul (the mediator between spirit and body), and physical body (the lower self or ego). You are always journeying through the soul between either your spirit (spirit-reigning) or physical (natural-reigning). The soul makes choices in every moment of your existence. The power of your choice is your authority in your life.

You are already living your life from your spirit, soul and body. Even if one believes or only focuses on the physical realm, the spiritual realm is still in motion. Attitude is present and operating in your tri-part self: spirit, soul and body.

Now that you have some insight regarding your true identity and tri-part self, journey from the inside out. Choose to align with the Word of God, the

Word of Love – it is the most powerful truth spoken with spiritual words. This is the part of you that God or Love communes with. Allow the attitude of Love to flow from you by choosing to walk lovingly, by choosing to talk lovingly, and by choosing to think loving thoughts toward your human family because we are all one. Choosing is the one thing we continuously do in every moment, whether we realize it or not. Imitate God or Love always.

Know that the attitude of love will manifest peace and joy, if you choose it, in every area of your life. God dwells in your spirit. In order to release God's attributes into the world, you simply choose to love in every moment, choose to align with the attitude of Love, and then Love's nature is released from your authentic self.

It is solely your choice.

THE BEGINNING

www.ingramcontent.com/pod-product-compliance
Lightning Source LLC
Chambersburg PA
CBHW061316040426
42444CB00010B/2676